# From My Heart, To Yours

## A Book of Inspirational Poetry & much more

*by Kat Dirato*

From My Heart, To Yours
ISBN: 978-0-6151-6750-3
Copyright © 2007 by Kat Dirato
Standard Copyright License
Language: English
Country: United States
Edition: First Edition
All Rights Reserved

# Acknowledgements

To my husband, Paul, you may not know it but you have been a true inspiration to me and I want to thank you for standing by my side and telling me I can do this. If it weren't for all your encouraging words, I couldn't have done it without you. So thank you for that and I will love you always!

To my Kasey, the poem I wrote for you was one of the first poems that I have written since High School, so I thank you for rekindling the fire that used to burn inside of me.

To my mom and dad, I want to thank you for all your support and for always answering the phone when I had a new poem to read, you always made me feel like a true poet!

To my mother in law, Carol, thank you also for listening and reading my poems and for all your kind words and for sharing my gift with others!

To my family and friends, who cheered for me from the sidelines, thank you all so much, I can't tell you how much it meant to me!

And of course, even though it goes without saying, my poetry is a true gift from God and I am so thankful to be so blessed with such a wonderful gift and that I am able to share it with others. I hope you enjoy reading my poetry as much as I enjoy writing it!

# Inspirational Poems

## Dear God

Am I all the things You expect me to be?
Each day I pray I grow closer to Thee
I know You know the way I feel
My life has been a journey and so surreal
Of course each day isn't perfect, that's true
But all that I am is because of You
You put love into my heart
that made an easy start
Learning so much throughout the years
Being the best I can be and have no fears
Be kind and compassionate, do unto others
Treat all that I meet, like my sisters and brothers
Remembering these words at the start of each day
Passing them on to all who come my way
Some days it's hard, to be all I should be
I try to remember the words You taught me
Those are the words that help me get through
"Do unto others, as you'd have done unto you"
"Don't let the sun go down upon your wrath"
"The Word is a lamp unto my feet
and a light unto my path"
A few valuable scriptures to know
Here is one more, "You reap what you sow"
Those words help me through each day
of course, remembering to pray
All I hope is that You are proud of me
I am all You expect me to be!
So when the final day does arrive
I know it's with You,
I will be eternally alive

## Time to Choose

When God came to me and told me its time
Time to choose your Mom and Dad
I knew it was you two I had to have
For there would be much love around me
I never imagined how "much" love there would be
From the minute you held me in your arms
I felt so safe and free from harm
Each passing year has been a blessing from above
You touched my heart and filled it with your love
There are so many things you taught me to be
To share and to love, be the best you can be
You instilled these from the very start
So many memories I hold within my heart
Many years have come and gone
I've grown and have a family of my own
A family I am blessed with
and so proud of
To them I will be sure
to pass on your love


~I Love You, Mom & Dad~

## Perfect Sacrifice

One day God was thinking of just what to do
He was so saddened by us
But how could He get through
then He thought of a perfect sacrifice
They have to believe, this is so concise
God became a man
So He could teach us how to live
He became our friend
So He could teach us to forgive
He wanted to make sure that we did our best
To believe in Him, no matter what the test
He wanted us to know we were created like Him
And it wasn't right for us to sin
He wanted us to know we were created to be
a part of His perfect family
He didn't think this was much to ask for
But we turned Him away, we closed the door
He showed us miracles, so we would believe
But we found it all so hard to conceive
He showed us the light, so our world was not so dim
But we just couldn't wait to "Crucify Him"
We hung Him on the cross
that wasn't suffice
We had to lot for His clothes
by throwing some dice
As He hung from the cross
He said "It is done"
Dying for us, God's beloved son
I did this for them because I love them so
I will always be here, when they want to know
why I was the perfect sacrifice
Just call out my name
It is "Jesus Christ"

## God's Child

You are so precious and oh so sweet
You bring so much joy to everyone you meet
You're so full of laughter, so full of love
for that we can thank the Lord above
I know you have been blessed with so many gifts
There's a special one, that's the spirits you lift
You are so full of smiles and cute little screams
I'm sure when you get older you'll have big dreams
Just remember to pray and ask God to help you
Whether it's big or small He will see you through~
Just follow your dreams and be sure to pray
Taking each step in life, living day by day
His word will tell you what he wants you to do
Each verse will clearly speak to you
This is one that speaks so loudly to me
You will find it Proverbs chapter three


**Proverbs 3:5**
Trust in the LORD with all thy heart; and
lean not unto thy own understanding.

## Walk in His Ways

We're on two different roads, you and I
In life these things happen, I'm not sure why
I pray some day we will meet up again
God's the only one who knows if we can
There are times in life we must go through a test
If we show Him we believe, He will handle the rest
It's so very painful to see you this way
And I thank God for giving me the strength to stay
Before things can get better, we need to agree
He comes first, that's the way it must be
All other things will be where they should
we will be rewarded with all that is good
It tells us this in the Bible, you'll find
Love Him with all your heart, soul and mind
Follow His commandments and walk in His ways
He shall take care of us all of our days
Until this happens, we must never doubt
For the Lord always provides us with a way out


### 1 Corinthians 10:13
No trial has come to you but what is human.
God is faithful and will not let you be tried
beyond your strength; but with the trial he will
also provide a way out, so that you may be able to bear it.

## Life's Road

We never know
where our road will lead
On this journey
we must plant many seeds
One thing's for certain, God does know
with these seeds, He will make us grow
Every day is like a blessing in disguise
with each passing day
He will make us wise
If we trust in Him
to guide us through each day
One step at a time, He will lead the way
Sometimes, He'll send an angel to help out
Whatever it may be, we can never doubt
For we know He is watching over His sheep
He would never want us lost or to see us weep
For before the womb,
we were His from the start
And He wants us to have
all the desires of our heart!

## Angels in Our Midst

We're each assigned an Angel
to guide us on our way
They're always watching over us
each and every day
God has sent them here
to fulfill many tasks
If we need help from our Angel
all we need to do is ask
Sometimes to do our Father's will
they will intercede
But only God knows
the things we really need

## Psalms 91:11-12
For He shall give his angels charge
over thee, to keep thee in all thy ways
They shall bear thee up in their hands,
lest thou dash thy foot against a stone

## His Promise

We love you and we are praying for you
Remember that God loves you, too
He will be there to take away your pain
To comfort you, when there's rough terrain
Sometimes things happen and we ask God "Why?"
He takes a deep breath and says with a sigh
Let your heart be not troubled, but believe in me
The day will come when you will see
All things work together
for My greater good
So that you may live eternally
as I promised you would
Even though you may not understand
Reach out in faith and take my hand
For if in My words you will abide
I will never leave you,
I'll always be by your side
When things in life
seem too hard to bare
Just remember
that I am "always" here

## Still Sinning

He gave us a mind
along with free will
But when satan knocks
we choose him still
Right from the beginning
we chose to sin
We continue to let
the prince of darkness in
From the book of Genesis
Adam and Eve
Listened to the serpent
so God made them leave
Why would we leave such a beautiful place
To live in shame, having to hide our face
Yes, the gate to destruction
is easy and wide
But God wants to see us,
He doesn't want us to hide
There is so much more
if we live by His word
He has treasures in store for us,
haven't you heard?
If we obey His commands
here on Earth
In heaven He will show us
what it is worth
But first we must obey
the sinning must cease
Then, with our Father
we can live eternally in peace

## Pentecost

Fifty days after Easter
we receive God's great power
Wind and flames of fire
the Holy Spirit came this hour
The disciples were locked in a room
together huddled in fear
Until Jesus came to them to tell them
what they needed to hear
He said "As my Father sent me,
so I am sending you
Receive the Holy Spirit
as I breath upon each of you
Now you are filled with the gifts
that have been promised to you
Go out and tell all the world
of what they now must do
Let them know there is forgiveness
of sins for all who believe
And that the Holy Spirit is there
for all of them to receive

## With You, Always

You're in a new place
it's sad but true
One thing's for sure
we will always love you
Yes, it was sad to see you go
We wish you blessings
more than you know
Things will work out
for the best you will see
Because God is with you
no matter where you might be
He will guide your path
and see you're okay
Leading you every step of the way
So trust in the Lord
with all your heart
He has been with you always
from the start

# F R I E N D S (Acrostic)

**F** inding a true friend is sometimes rare
**R** elying on someone who truly does care
**I** f you find this special person, let them know
**E** specially how much they mean, don't let go
**N** ever forget the importance of a friend
**D** on't ever let a good friendship end

**F** inding a true friend is a rare find
**R** elying on someone who is true but kind
**I** f you do find someone like this in your journey
**E** ach day with your friend will be special, you'll see
**N** ever let friendship become a thing in the past
**D** on't ever give up, make sure that it lasts

**F** riendship is a great thing to share
**R** emember your friends and show them you care
**I** t means so much just knowing they're there
**E** ven at times when they can't be near
**N** ever underestimate the power of a friend
**D** ecide to stay together until the very end

## M A R R I A G E (Acrostic)

**M** arriage is love, it joins you together
**A** nd when this happens, you can storm any weather
**R** emember this, let love be your guide
**R** espect each other, stand by each other's side
 **I** n all things, ask God what to do
**A** nd He will be sure to see you through
**G** iving you guidance and a path to walk along
**E** ndure in love, for each day is like a song

## Wedding Day

To each other you have made a special vow
Let the Lord see you through it now
From this day forward until the end
It is He in which you can depend
You may come across a Mountain or two
the Lord will be sure to see you through
Never be discouraged
and never doubt
He will make sure
you have a way out
Some roads may seem to never end
But remember,
it is He in which you can depend
So love one another in every way
Be good to each other every day
if you need help along the way
Get down on your knees
and begin to pray
For you have made a vow,
till death do you part
The Lord is with you always
Just look into your heart

## In Season

I believe God brought us
together for a reason
All good things happen
in the right season
But I think we need
to prove ourselves first
To show God it's
His word that we thirst
When He believes
we are ready to commit
Not go halfway
and then say that we quit
That's when the seed
will begin to grow
That's when all of God's love
for us will show

## A Sad September Day

It was so hard to watch the news that day
Over and over they had to play and replay
The chills that went through my body, how I cried
So many loved ones on that horrible day died
It will be a day we will never forget
to think it's still not over yet
Do you think God looks down, in disgust
and wonders why He ever created us?
He made us out of love and gave us free will
So many of us choose to hate and to kill
This is such a sad world that we must live in
Not even giving a second thought about sin
Do you remember how we pulled together on 9/11
Praying for our loved ones who are now in heaven
Candlelit vigils and praying every day
Then slowly we slipped back to our old ways
Why do we find it so hard to do good
Living the way that God said we should
We are His people
He loves each and every one
He proved it by giving up His only Son
So live each day, as if the end was coming fast
Remembering those who didn't know
that day would be their last

**In Memory of Those**
**Who Were Taken**
**On September 11, 2001**

## A Life Taken

Our children only know
the things that they are taught
Some think it's ok
if they just don't get caught
They say "it's okay
I'm fine to drive"
Taking a chance
to make it home alive
On their way home
they start to think
"What am I doing?
I've had too much to drink"
Right at that moment
it becomes too late
On that dark road
a life is lost to fate
There's no going back
no changing it, you see
A life was taken
because you turned the key
Now a family grieves
they lost their loved one
You're saying to yourself
"What have I done?"
And I'm sure not once
did the thought cross your mind
That, on this fatal night
You'd be the one outlined

**~Don't Drink & Drive~**

## Getting Through

Thank you Father
for helping me through
It was difficult for me
though I kept my faith in you
There were times when I doubted
and told you so
You stayed by my side
and helped me to know
That my feelings were normal
it's how we were made
If I continued to believe
those feelings would fade
So each morning I woke
and gave thanks to you
I prayed the things
that you taught me to
I kept strong in my faith
and didn't doubt
That you would guide me
and show me a way out
So Father, I praise you
for your wondrous deeds
For helping me through
when I was in need

## Wait upon the Lord

Life is so wonderful
I feel truly blessed
Even though there are times
when put to the test
Believing in the Father
and listening to His voice
Are the things He asks
so we make the right choice
He will be with us always,
He promised us so
I will instruct thee
in which way to go
This is written in the Bible
Psalms 32 verse 8
He will lead us to righteousness
for His name's sake
There will be difficult times
we are not alone
He promised us a helper
The One who was called to His throne
So when things seem hard
and you're not sure why
Wait upon the Lord
He has heard your cry

### Psalm 32:8
I will instruct you and show you the way you should walk,
give you counsel and watch over you.

### "Why Me, God?"

In life, we all bare
some pain or trial
Some seem easy,
but some last awhile
and we wonder,
"Why God, I don't understand"
Then He whispers,
"Reach out & take my hand,
Trials in life
are what make you strong
if you have faith,
I will help you along
Yes, there may be times
when you feel helpless and scared
and this trial is something
you can no longer bare
But remember I am with you
each step of the way"
My love for you will get you
through each & every day

## Surrender

God created us
for His many pleasures
So we may receive
His promised treasures
All He asks for
is our love and our trust
But we turn away
"Shame on us"
Stripping our country
of all its beliefs
So that sinners
can feel a little relief
Our founding fathers
expressed to the nation
Religious faith
is the true foundation
So let's build ourselves up
and make it our goal
To please the Lord
with our heart, mind and soul
You can be as close to Him
as you choose
By surrendering yourself
you will never lose

## Smile for Me

My life here on earth
was a wonderful one
I lived life to the fullest
but now it is done
It's time to move on
To complete other tasks
It's what I must do
it's what God asks
So please don't be sad
and do not cry
Do not question
asking God "why"?
For there's no more suffering
and no more pain
Just the warmth of the sun
and the mist from the rain
It's the place we were promised
where all things are new
This is the place
that I have gone to
The water is pure and
crystal clear
There is nothing here
we need to fear
The walls are garnished
in precious stone
My father in heaven
has called me home
So smile for me
until we meet again
Love to you all
my family & friends

## Angels on Earth

Sometimes we feel sad
and a little blue
We don't know why
or how to get through
That's why God
made wonderful friends
He knew what He was doing
and He knew who to send
To cheer us up
when we're down & out
to make us smile, instead of pout
They are called "Angels"
here on earth
and He knew what their help
to us would be worth

# SPECIAL POEMS
# SPECIAL OCCASIONS

## The One

From the second I saw you
I knew you were the one
With you I would spend today,
tomorrow
and all the years to come
I want you to know
you mean the world to me
If it weren't for you
I would not be me
You have inspired me to do
many things in my life
And it makes me so proud
to be your wife


**~I Love You, Paul ~**

## Kasey Rose

I thank the Lord every night
For giving me such a beautiful sight
She has her Daddy's eyes
her Mommy's nose
She's my little girl,
My Kasey Rose
She brings me such joy
both day and night
Each morning she wakes
and hugs me so tight
She means so very much to me
She's my sunrise, my sunset
My favorite melody
I thank you God for blessing me so
What she means to me
only you can know
I can't wait for the mornings to arrive
To see her face
makes me feel so alive
You have sent to me
an Angel in Disguise
So I thank you Father,
again and again
For blessing me
with my daughter,
my Best Friend

## Baptism

Being baptized
is very special, you see
Being a follower of Jesus
is what you will be
Your Mom and Dad
will show you the way
You can be sure they will help you
each and every day
Teaching you things
that Jesus would do
To love one another
as God loves you
You will learn these things
as you grow
Little by little
you will get to know
God created us
to be part of His family
To become like His Son
is how he wants us to be
So as you are blessed
on this very special day
Just follow Jesus
He will show you the way

## Blessed Sacrament

Holy Communion is a special time
Receiving Jesus in bread and wine
His body has been broken and
His blood has been shed
For forgiveness of sins
Is why Jesus bled
At the Last Supper
He made us a promise
That when we receive Him
He will be in us
We are to do this
In "Remembrance of Him"
To keep us strong
To keep us from sin
So when you receive
the "Blessed Sacrament"
Remember it is Jesus
whom, for us, God sent

## He is Risen

Lent is the time of year
Where all things become anew
Christ died on the cross and
He did this all for you
So as you journey
Through this season
Remember the purpose
Remember the reason
I know sometimes it's hard
Sometimes we may forget
that's why God sent His Son
He came to pay our debt
So show Him how much you love Him
Don't let his sufferings go in vain
And on the last day you'll be with Him
In His triumphant reign


Christ has risen on this day
Conquering death & paying our way
Thanks be to God
for sending His Son
He has risen
Now it is done

## Valentines Day

We have been blessed
with the gift of love
And this gift has come
from God above
He put this love
within our hearts
It's always been there
from the start
His commandments were to love Him
with our heart, mind and soul
And to love one another
is what we were told
so show your love not only today
but throughout the year
each and every day

## To My Valentine

I'm so happy
that you are mine
Yes it's true,
I have the BEST valentine
It must have been
my turn to be blessed
God put us together
and we became one flesh
To me,
that was the best day of my life
The day we became
husband and wife
I love you more
with each passing day
and together forever
is how we will stay

**To Our Valentine Girl**

Kasey Rose,
you're our valentine girl
The bestest valentine
in the whole world
We love you so very much
When God sent you to us
Our lives were touched
Because he sent us the very best
Since you've been our valentine
Our lives have been blessed

**We Love You, Kasey**

## A True Gift

God made mother's
special indeed
They are what He calls
a rare breed
For they are there
both day and night
To comfort their children
and hold them tight
Loving them
no matter what the cost
Taking them back
when they are lost
Sitting through concerts
or plays they are in
Watching their games
whether they lose or win
Letting them know
a job's been well done
But what's important
is that they had fun
Catching them
if they stumble and fall
Or just to talk
whenever they call
When they are down
their spirits we lift
Yes, being a mother
is a precious gift
So cherish your children
whether big or small
Because being a Mom
is the best gift of all

## Do Your Best

Being a Mom
is a hard job, I think
They grow up so fast
be sure not to blink
My daughter just turned
eleven this year
Her turning eighteen
is what I fear
I pray I am teaching her
what she needs to know
when the time comes for her to go
Will she know which direction
and head the right way?
Will she remember the things
that I had to say?
These are the questions
on my mind
All I can do is pray
she will find
If she listens carefully
and follows her heart
Good things will happen
from the start
So, if you're a Mom
I'm sure you feel the same way
Just do the best that you can
don't forget to pray
Asking God to help you along
With Him on your side,
you can't go wrong

**Happy Mother's Day
To My Mom**

I just want to say thanks
for all that you do
There are so many things
I've learned from you
now I can pass them on
to my little girl
So she can be prepared
to go out in the world
Thank you so much
for all your love and care
and most of all
for "Always" being there!

**I Love You, Mom 5/05**

## A Father

To the Fathers out there
who give it their all
Working hard all day
then you come home and play ball
Or just being there
Teaching them right from wrong
To be a leader with their friends
be the one who is strong
It may seem like they're not listening
but they hear what you say
so continue to be there
day after day
because a Father's role
is an important one
Whether you're raising a daughter
or raising a son
Children need their dads
it's a known fact
A Father is what keeps
the family intact

## To My Daddy

I just want you to know
how much I love you
and thank you
for all the things that you do
Like taking me on the boat
or motorcycle rides
Spending time with you
makes me feel good inside
Daddy to me,
you are a hero in my eyes
I look up to you
because you are so wise
You're the best dad
in the whole wide world
and I'm so glad
I'm "your" little girl
I guess we both got lucky that way
I love you so much, Dad
Happy Father's Day!

**Happy Father's Day
To My Dad**

Thank you, Dad,
for all that you do
I hope you know
how much I love you!
You are always there,
no matter what time of day
I know I can count on you
in every way
Like the card says,
"You are pretty rare"
So thanks again, Dad,
for always being there!

**I Love You, Dad 5/05**

## Happy Father's Day

You're the best Dad
I know this is true
because no one can compete
with a Dad like you
You are always there
when I need you the most
Having you as a Dad
makes me wanna boast
You always have time
when it comes to me
Thanks for all that you do
and for being my Daddy!

## The Best Dad in the World

You are my dad
and it's make me so proud
I want to shout it out
into the crowd
You've always been there
and for that, I love you
I couldn't have been blessed
with a better Dad than you!

## Memorial Day

We seem to have forgetten
of what this day is for
It's to honor those men & women
who have died in war
Not just a long weekend
of fun and celebration
But to remember those who died
defending our nation
They fought for our freedom
and here they now lay
So let's not forget about them
this Memorial Day
At 3 pm, stop what you're doing
and pause
Remembering those soldiers
who died for a cause
When they look down from heaven
they will see us unified
For we are thankful for our freedom
the very reason they died

## Independence Day

The Fourth of July is also known
as Independence day
Because we were joined
by France & Spain
We have our freedom now today
Lady Liberty stands proud & tall
In the bay of New York Harbour
In one hand she holds a book of law
and a torch is raised up by her
The broken shackles
that lay at her feet
Is the very proof
America can't be beat
In 1776 our Independence was made secure
Let's not forget the ones who fought
and all that they endured

## Happy Birthday

Today is your birthday
a special day indeed
God made you special
and inside there's a seed
A seed that must grow
to accomplish his tasks
So be sure to be ready
to do what God asks
If you listen real close
He will let you know
which seeds to plant
so your harvest will grow
He wants you to have
all the desires of your heart
These are the promises
he made from the start
So rejoice in God
on this very special day
and He will bless you
each step of the way

**To Our Kasey Rose**
**on her 10<sup>th</sup> Birthday**
**3/28/06**

Where did ten wonderful years go?
Can you tell me where, do you know?
I can tell you that
they went by so fast
But the memories of them
will always last
God entrusted you to us
and put you in our care
He knew what would happen
by placing you here
The amount of love
that there would be
Only He could know,
only He could foresee
So we thank you Father
for the blessings from above
and for our girl, Kasey,
who's brought us so much love

**Happy 1ˢᵗ Birthday**
**To Mikey 11/05**

Time sure does fly
when you are having fun
I can't believe
you are turning one
It seems like just yesterday
you were a little guy
Now you're blowing kisses
and waving bye-bye
Once you start walking,
there's no stopping you
You'll be talking in sentences,
saying "I love you"
But the very best part,
I want you to know
Is I will be there
watching you grow


**Happy 2ⁿᵈ Birthday**
**To Mikey 11/06**

Boy oh Boy…Time sure flies fast
I can't believe 2 years have past
We hope your day is a special one
With lots of cake and lots of fun!!

## Happy Thanksgiving

It is on this day
we give thanks and praise
For God has blessed us
in special ways
We express the feelings
we have in our hearts
and implore Him to bless us
as each day starts
So let us come together
as God wants us to
and give thanks for his blessings,
good health & good food

~Amen~

## Our Christmas Miracle

Christmas is such a special day
Christ was born so we could say
Forgive me Father
for what I've done
Thank you for sending
your beloved Son
Christ was born
so we could be forgiven
Christ died
so we can continue living
So during this blessed
time of year
Let us not forget
of why we are here
Show others the same love
God has shown
By welcoming others
into your heart and home
Share your blessings
and your gifts from above
And you will be blessed
with so much more than His love

## A Child is Born

It's Christmas, once again
a very special time
So let's remember Christ
He's in our hearts
and in our minds
It's not about the gifts
the lights or even the tree
But how we treat each other
we're all part of God's family
So make sure you follow Jesus
He is the light and the way
He was sent to save us all
on this blessed Christmas Day

**Happy New Year**

Another New Year
is about to start
I wish you all
the desires of your heart
May it be full of prosperity
and full of wealth
But most importantly
may you have good health!

**Happy 1ˢᵗ Birthday
To Joshua 2/06**

Happy Birthday Joshua….Wow
We can't believe you're one now
You have brought so much happiness
to our home
We can't believe
how much you've grown
It seems like yesterday
You were such a little guy
We can't believe
a year has gone by
But the best part is
We want you to know
Being part of your life
and watching you grow

## Goodbye

Sometimes we lose our loved ones
without a chance to say goodbye
Then we start to wonder
and ask God, "Why"?
He says "There's a bigger picture
one you do not see
One day you'll understand
of why it had to be"
Just know your loved one is close
and will always be near
So say what's in your heart
for they will always hear
And for the time being
that you are apart
You can hold the
memories you have
deep within your heart

## A Baby Boy

How wonderful it is
You're having a boy
He will bring you much love
He will bring you much joy
The feelings you're feeling deep inside
You won't be able to contain
You won't be able to hide
All the "first" little things that he will do
First step, first word, first tooth too
Will make you smile with heartfelt joy
How wonderful it is your having a boy

## A Baby Boy

Congratulations
on your new little one
God has blessed you
with a beautiful son
A bundle of joy,
a baby boy
Tiny little hands,
tiny little feet
Baby breath
and baby heartbeats
This little baby boy,
we can't wait to meet

## A Baby Girl

How wonderful it is
you're having a girl
You will come to find
she's the center of your world
She will bring so much joy
into your hearts
From the moment she is placed
in your arms, it will start
So prepare yourselves
for this Blessed Event
God has chosen you
for this child to be sent

## A Baby Girl

God Bless you both
and your little girl
As she enters into
a whole new world
You will see her
and feel butterflies
Hearing her breath
and hearing her sighs
Nothing will be able
to take the place
Of what you're feeling
when you see her
sweet face

·

## Logan Jack James

A beautiful baby
is about to be born
He will be blessed
he will be adorned
How wonderful it is
for this little boy
He has no idea
he'll give so much joy
From the second he is placed
in your arms to be held
It will feel as though
you are under a spell
He has no idea
of the love he'll receive
When you look into his eyes,
you'll hardly believe
You'll try to remember
how you ever lived
Without this precious boy,
this precious gift

## Connor Anthony Hurley

A mommy and daddy
you're about to be
A little baby boy,
how lucky is he
To have not only the two of you
But he will have a big brother too
Now there will be diapers
that need to be changed
And your schedules
will need to be re-arranged
Nights will come
when the floor you will pace
But when you look
into that sweet babies face
Somehow
it all becomes worth it and more
And you'll wonder
"what was it like before?"
Before you were sent
this bundle of joy
This sweet little baby,
your baby boy

## Bear
### (To the Viscardi's)

The very first day
he didn't know what to do
He became my shadow
and broke my shoe
The second day
he was more at ease
He loved to follow Barney
and be a tease
We found that he loves
to lick his feet
And did you know that he snores
when he sleeps?
Having Bear this week
was lots of fun
He loved to go out back
and run and run
I even think
a few pounds he shed
Cuz' this morning
he jumped up onto our bed
Lo and behold the bed did not break
Even though I gave him a piece of cake
Ha ha, just kidding I was really good
I didn't give him any table food
So now that this week is over and done
And having Bear was lots of fun
If you ever need us
to watch him again
Barney says
"Cool, cuz Bear is my Friend!"

### 25 Years and Counting

How could 25 years go by so fast?
It's so nice to see true love can last
So many memories from so long ago
I remember the day you brought home Joe
He had one foot with a flip flop & one in a cast
It's so nice to see true love can last
I remember the day you left for overseas
It broke my heart to see you leave
But the letters, the pictures & cassettes you sent
I can't even tell you how much they meant
Then the day you called with such great news
I don't think mom and dad were amused
But I was thrilled, an aunt I would become
I couldn't wait for you to come home
The day finally came to see you at last
To see that your belly had grown so fast
A beautiful baby girl, then a chubby little boy
They both brought us so much joy
Now they are grown, and no longer home
Taking on the world day by day
Now you are grandparents, what can I say?
It's the circle of life, how it goes so fast
But love is the answer to making it last
Now a final word to both you and Joe
Paul and I want to thank you so
Because of you, we two have met
And although we haven't made 25 years yet
We look at you and have learned so much
Because of you our lives have been touched

**We Love You, Patty & Joe**
**May you be blessed another 25 years**

## Mr. Catrillo

I am writing this poem
to let you know
I am very sad to see you go
I have known you since
my first day of school
And I want you to know
I think you're cool
Your words of wisdom
always made my day
I always looked forward
to what you had to say
You're funny and nice
and you sing good too
These are the things
I will miss about you
I hope the new kids
know how lucky they are
They're getting the best principal,
it's YOU, by far

## Mr. Baker

I am writing this poem
to welcome you
And also to say
good luck, too
I think you will like it
here at our school
The past four years
have been really cool
The teachers and staff
are lots of fun
I think our school
is number one
So best of luck
from here on out
And if you need any help,
just give me a shout

## Mr. Guida

You taught me a lot of new things
in third grade
There were so many projects
and neat things we made
Reading in class
was one of my favorites of all
And writing in cursive
when we did D.O.L.
I loved going to Philly
to see the Human Heart
The Franklin Institute,
was my favorite part
Those are just
a few things that were fun
But having you as my teacher
was the best one

## Mrs. Diokmedjian

You're a great teacher
and I'll miss you a lot
I'll never forget
all the cool things you taught
Learning the planets
was a lot of fun
Of course, Saturn
was my favorite one
I also liked learning
about things in the ocean
Like coral reefs, anemones
and sea urchins
There are so many things
you taught me, it's true
I'll always remember 3$^{rd}$ grade
thanks to You!

## Miss Kruger

You made 5$^{th}$ grade a year
I'll never forget
You're the best teacher
that I've had yet
You taught us many things
in really fun ways
My favorite was writing
topic essays
Then there were the field trips
they were a lot of fun
The Philly trip, of course
was my favorite one
Well I hope your class next year
is a fun one too
I hope they know how lucky they are
to have a teacher like you!

## Patty & Joe

We are sending you on
a vacation in the sun
A place where you can relax
and have some fun
To rekindle your love
with the stars up above
To do whatever
your hearts desire
Sit on the beach
at night with a fire
Or take a long walk
hand in hand
Wiggle your toes
in the soft white sand
Swim in the ocean
that's such a beautiful blue
Whatever it is
you choose to do
Will make us so happy
because we love you
So enjoy every minute
and have lots of fun
And when you return
tell us all that you've done

## Father Jack

I believe God sent you to us, it's true
I feel He knew our parish needed you
We have been so blessed
with all that you've done
Our church is becoming more like one
I know we have quite a way to go
But having you here
is greater than you know
Each time you speak
my heart is opened
Capturing your words
that come from within
It's been a long time
since I've felt this way
Your powerful words,
and messages conveyed
You truly have been blessed
with a wonderful gift
There are so many hearts
and spirits you lift
I'm so glad that God
has answered our prayers
He sent us someone wonderful,
someone who cares
So, I just want to thank you
for "all" that you do
We're so glad you're here Father,
welcome, to you

**In Memory of Our Pal, Barney**
**9/14/91 – 5/6/05**

My buddy, my boo, my little boy
You always brought me so much joy
It's going to be sad not having you around
Saying, "Barney, please, Go sit down"
Not having you here to greet me at the door
To see what I bought for you at the store
You were always sure to brighten my day
And the only one who listened
to what I had to say
I knew I could always count on you
To cheer me up when I was feeling blue
I will definitely miss you cuddling with me
jumping into bed, when daddy would leave
Dropping the popcorn
for you on the floor
You'd follow me around
until I gave you more
When you knew I was sad
you'd give me a kiss
That's just the beginning
of the things I will miss
The house feels so empty
it's quiet without you
You will always be my boy,
my buddy, my boo
I look forward
to the day we meet again
To cross over Rainbow Bridge with you,
My boo, my best friend!

**To Barney from Kasey**

It's hard not having you around anymore
I still look for you
when I come through the door
From the day I was born,
you were always there
Making sure I was safe
and felt no fear
When I cried, you would pace
then give me a kiss
That's the one thing about you
I surely do miss
You made me laugh so hard
sometimes I would cry
The way you ran around
after your bath, to get dry
I loved throwing the ball for you to get
I've never seen a dog faster than you, yet
Playing hide and seek
was so much fun
Watching you lay on the deck,
taking in the sun
I'm so thankful of the memories
that I have with you
Like when you sang "Happy Birthday"
and other songs, too
In my heart,
you will always have a special place
Because you always made sure
to put a smile on my face

### To Baby ... 7/18/05

You were the prettiest girl I ever met
I've never seen a prettier dog yet
Your eyes were so cool,
like you wore black eyeliner
I've never seen a dog look any finer
That sleek little body
and shiny fur
All the other girl dogs saying
"I wish I was her"
But they can keep wishin',
it won't come true
Cuz' there will never be
a girl any finer than you!
Baby, we'll miss you,
not having you here
Please do me a favor,
take care of Barney up there!

## Brutis

I remember when we met
It was down the shore
You came running to me
when I walked through the door
You were clumsy
and falling all over the place
I loved those puppy kisses
all over my face
Then you grew and you grew
you got so big
Your favorite past time
was to dig and dig
Barking at the squirrels
in the backyard
You were the boss
it was your job to guard
There were some
who did fear
But to me you were
abig teddy bear
It's hard to believe
you're no longer here
But I know you're having fun
with Barney, up there!

## Happy Halloween

It's Halloween,
a spooky time of year
Black cats, witches and goblins,
all the things that scare
Spine chilling music
and creepy ghosts sounds too
It's fun to see the costumes
and try to guess who's who???
Candy, candy, candy…
that's the best part for sure
So grab your bag
and let's go knock on everyone's door

## Ode to Paul Carolla

What you did for us
means more than you know
And the Lord will make sure
you reap what you sow
We know you didn't do it
for that reason
But all good things come
in the right season
Your harvest will be
in abundance, it's true
We are so grateful, Paul
may God Bless You!

## To Eleni & Her Family

This weekend was great
we had lots of fun
We want to say thanks
for all that you've done
You're friendship to us
means so very much
Since we've been friends
our lives have been touched
True friendship can sometimes
be a rare find
But the friendship we have
is one of a kind

## A Simple Thanks

I just wanted to say thanks
for all that you do
You were always there
when I needed you
No matter what it was
you took the time out
To help me through
when I was in doubt
So thank you again
for helping me through
The worlds a better place
because of you

## John Somma
## (J & N Service Station)

I just want to tell you
how thankful we are
You came through for us
like a shining star
I know the task
wasn't an easy one
But you made sure
you got it done
Your hard work means
more than you know
Some day, you will
reap what you sow
Even though it wasn't done
for that reason
All good things come
in the right season
So thank you again
for all that you've done
May your harvest in life
be a plentiful one

## To My Friends

Thanks 4 sharing
in my special night
and making my "40th" birthday
just right
As you all know,
I had a blast
I can't believe
the night went so fast
I wish it could have
gone on forever
Because for me,
that was the best birthday ever

## To My Special Friend

Thank you for all the things you do
But most of all for being you
I knew we would be
best of friends
Never letting
our friendship end
It takes hard work
to make a friendship last
And not let it become
a thing of the past
I believe that's what
the two of us share
And I wanted to tell you,
Thanks for being there!

I Love you, Debbie~

### Juanita, My Bonita

I want to thank you
for all that you do
I'm so lucky
to have a friend like you
You're always there
showing you care
You're thoughtful, kind
and lovable, too
God blessed me
with a great friend
It's You!

## To Our Armed Forces
## Many Special Thanks

To the men and women
who serve our country
Living a disciplined life,
so we can be free
There's no way we can ever
repay what you do
but we want you to know
how much we thank you
we are praying for you
night and day
that the time will come soon
and they will say
Your job is now done
and you can go
Home to your families
who miss you so!

## Happy Anniversary

Can you believe how fast
the years have gone by
When you're having fun
time will surely fly
I just want you to know
for me it has been fun
You're my true love
my friend, my only one
There's nobody else
I'd rather have in my life
Like I told you before
I'm proud to be your wife
And I know the next 15
will be just as great
We belong together
we are soul mates

~Paul & Kat 4ever~

**Happy Anniversary**

It seems like only yesterday
You walked into my life
It seems like only yesterday
we became husband & wife
We've made so many memories
in these past 16 years
Some brought lots of smiles &
Yes, some brought tears
But I wouldn't trade it
for all the world
Because you're my guy
and I'll "always" be your girl

## Cujo & Watson

Cujo you were a Sheltie, black & white
Because of you,
we couldn't sleep with mom at night
Watson for once,
you hit the nail on the head
But there were many nights
when I snuck into her bed
and at least I didn't chase my tail
I wasn't a seeing-eye dog that failed
Ok, Cujo you got me there, I must admit
But at least I listened to mom
when she told me to sit
Not always trying to be a big shot
Or trying to be something I'm not
Cuz' ya know inside you were a big mush
And when I tried to tell mom you'd say "shush"
Alright Watson, that may be true
But I had to be tough for mom and you
Now that it's out, I just have to say
I'm glad we're together & we can play
Until we meet up with mom again
She will always be "Our Best Friend"

### You're Engaged

Congratulations
on your Engagement
To each other, by God,
you have been sent
You were chosen to become
husband & wife
To bring happiness & love
into each others life
Remember
on the blessed day,
when the words "I Do"
are what you say
You are now one
Instead of two
May God Bless
the both of you

### Remember Them

Veteran's Day, to me,
seems to go unrecognized
But we owe it to the soldiers
for the freedom in our lives
They paid a price of blood and sweat
Laying in mud cold and wet
Without any shelter or food for days
Underneath the sun's sweltering rays
I can't even imagine how a soldier feels
How each day he copes
and how each day he deals
Wondering when
the enemy's next attack will be
Will he make it home
to see his family
What other thoughts
must go through their mind
How they would feel
if they had to leave a friend behind
Being a soldier to me, is very scary indeed
But I understand it's what our country needs
The freedom that was fought for
many years before
Still has to be protected
still worth fighting for
So Thank you to "Our Troops"
for being so very brave
May Our American Flag,
in your honor, always wave!

**Let's show our appreciation for what our soldiers do
By honoring them not only today, but the whole year through**

## A Day to Remember

This is a day you'll never forget
But the best part hasn't begun yet
Tomorrow you will start the rest of your life
When you wake in the morning
you'll be husband & wife
Ready for adventures
and a new journey ahead
This all started
with the vows you have said
To love and to honor each other, you will
Whether it's a mountain ahead or a little hill
The important part is you do it together
Believe in your heart things will get better
be sure that you stand side by side
Remain in God's love, remember to abide
He is the one who will see you through
As He gently guides the both of you
To the things He has prepared for you lives
From this day
when you became Husband & Wife

**God Bless You Both, John & Stacy**

## Graduation Day

You're graduating,
Ah, at last
But to us this day
came too fast
You became a woman
right before our eyes
So mature and oh so wise
We knew all along
this day would arrive
Sending you off
so you could strive
To figure out in life
What you want to be
Maybe to start
your own family
No matter what it is
you choose to do
We want you to know
we are so proud of you

## Your New Home

May your new home be blessed
by God above
May it be filled with warmth
and lots of love
May all who come to visit you
be guarded and protected too
May memories be made
that make you smile
May angels be with you
all the while

## Another Milestone

You're 40 now
and have accomplished so much
But most importantly
are the lives that you've touched
You're always there
to lend a helping hand
Even though your life
has its own demands
You're thoughtful
caring and generous too
Which is why you are loved
by many, it's true
So I just want to say "thanks"
for being my friend
And here's to "Our Friendship"
May it never end!


**Happy Birthday, Diane**

**Nadine**
**1995-2007**

Nadine, you were with us
for many years
Even though right now
it's hard to hold back the tears
I'll never forget your first visit up
You were so little, you were just a pup
you and Barney would play with each other
You got along so well, like you were sister and brother
Outside he would run around and around
Then you'd put out your paw and swat him down
There are so many memories we have of you
So many funny things that you would do
Like pushing your food out all over the floor
Or when you wanted a treat you'd hit the cabinet door
Dribbling and slobbering, the floor would be soaked
if Grammy saw it hanging, it would make her choke
Those things are just to name a few
Of why we are going to miss you
But I have to say, it's a comfort to me
Knowing, once again, you'll be with Barney
Playing together the way you used to
Goodbye, Nadine, we love you

**Goodbye to Bear**
**The Last of "Our" Clan**
**2/27/07**

Bear you will be greatly missed
I didn't know you well
But I am sure of this
You were always so friendly
and so so sweet
When I came to visit
you'd sit by my feet
Like a big cuddly teddy bear
This news was very sad to hear
But I know you are young at heart again
Playing in heaven with all "our" best friends

# Leader of the Pack

Our trip started out with a flat tire
but at least it wasn't anything dire
Thank God for the overpass
and the chalk that we found
We were out of the sun
and played hopscotch, one round
Then finally our "Tow Woman" saved the day
We were off, and on our way
To a wonderful place called the Chocolate Café
The people were nice and the food was great
But we had to go, our arrival would be late
Maryland was where we were headed to
And on the way, what a beautiful view
We made it to the motel, it was just about nine
Freshened up, changed, then went out to dine
Sunday came, we headed towards DC
but the traffic was further than we could see
So, West Virginia, we were bound
To see Harpers Ferry and the raid of John Brown
Made it back to the motel before the rain came down heavy
And when it was over we walked over to Chevy's
It was Mexican that night and Tequila too
And I promised John I would wear the right shoes
The next morning came and we tried DC again
Even though Susan wanted to sleep in
But we made it there and got to see a lot
Even though the walking was much and it was hot
There was one place that had a huge impact on me
The Holocaust Memorial is a must see
Back to the bikes and we hit the highway
John & Sheri, I must say
This weekend was fun and we had a blast
And as usual it always goes too fast
But the next time you want to be Leader of the Pack
Just say the word and our bags will be packed!

Love Always ~ Kat & Paul

**Ryan & Amanda**

Love one another,
as you have been loved
This is a commandment
by God above
On this day,
two became one
A wonderful Journey
has just begun
Live life to the fullest
every day
Lift each other up
along the way
And you will see
God's plan unfold
Your lives together,
will be more precious
than gold